TUPAC SHAKUR

CARRIE GOLUS

In Consultation with Martha Cosgrove,
M.A. and Reading Specialist

JUST THE FACTS BIOGRAPHIES

LERNER PUBLICATIONS COMPANY/MINNEAPOLIS

Martha Cosgrove has a master's degree from the University of Minnesota in secondary education, with an emphasis on developmental and remedial reading. She is licensed in 7–12 English and language arts, developmental reading, and remedial reading. She has had several works published, and she gives numerous state and national presentations in her areas of expertise.

Lerner Publications Company
A division of Lerner Publishing Group
241 First Avenue North
Minneapolis, Minnesota U.S.A.

Website address: www.lernerbooks.com

Library of Congress Cataloging-in-Publication Data

Golus, Carrie, 1969–
    Tupac Shakur : by Carrie Golus in consultation with Martha Cosgrove.
      p. cm. — (Just the facts biographies)
    Includes bibliographical references and index.
    ISBN-13: 978–0–8225–6609–0 (lib. bdg. : alk. paper)
    ISBN-10: 0–8225–6609–5 (lib. bdg. : alk. paper)
    1. Shakur, Tupac, 1971–1996–Juvenile literature. 2. Rap musicians–
United States–Biography–Juvenile literature. I. Cosgrove, Martha. II. Title.
ML3930.S48G65 2007
782.421649092–dc22 [B]   2006028365

Manufactured in the United States of America
1 2 3 4 5 6 – DP – 12 11 10 09 08 07

CONTENTS

CHAPTER 1

HOW LONG WILL THEY MOURN ME?

The murder of Tupac Shakur (above) in 1996 affected many people, especially young African Americans.

LAS VEGAS, NEVADA, was burning hot on Friday, September 13, 1996. Outside the University Medical Center, a small crowd sweated. The temperature soared to one hundred degrees. The group was mostly young, mostly African American. There were dozens of children. They were there because of Tupac Shakur, the rapper as famous for his police record as for his music. Inside the hospital, Tupac was fighting for his life.

Six days before, Tupac had been shot four times. He had been riding in a car driven by Marion "Suge" Knight. Knight was a close friend. He also owned Death Row Records, Tupac's record label. At a stoplight, a white Cadillac pulled up next to Knight's car. Someone inside opened fire. Tupac was hit twice in the chest, once in the hand, and once in the leg. Knight wasn't seriously hurt.

Marion "Suge" Knight walks past the crowd into the Las Vegas hospital where Tupac was fighting for his life.

Still, few people thought Tupac would die. He had already survived one shooting two years before. That time, he took five bullets. Two of them were to the head. And yet he had checked himself out of the hospital the very same day. "I haven't seen anybody in my twenty-five-year . . . career leave the hospital like this," Dr. Leon Pachter, one of Tupac's surgeons, had told reporters afterward.

But the Las Vegas shooting was much more serious. Knight and Tupac's mother, Afeni, were at the hospital. Tupac couldn't get out of bed. On his third day, doctors took out his right lung. On his sixth day, they gave him drugs to put him into a coma (deep sleep). They did so to keep him from trying to get out of bed and hurting himself. On the seventh day, he gave up the fight. Tupac died at 4:03 P.M. He was twenty-five years old.

"If I Die 2night"

News of Tupac's death spread quickly. The crowd outside the hospital grew larger. Many of the mourners wept. Some stared blankly into space. Others spilled liquor on the ground in Tupac's honor. A long line of cars circled the area.

Many of them blasted Tupac's music. The most popular songs were those about death, such as "If I Die 2night."

Afeni Shakur left the hospital, surrounded by family. Knight showed no emotion as he pushed through the crowd. There was just one moment of anger. A friend of Tupac's screamed at the hospital staff. He demanded to know why they'd let Tupac die.

Hundreds of police officers made sure the mourning stayed peaceful. But there was no violence. There was just a feeling of deep sadness. "I hope you tell the truth about Tupac," one young mourner told a reporter for *Rolling Stone*. "He was a hero to me, and he kept it real for the hood [neighborhood]."

SON OF A PANTHER

Tupac's mother was a leader in the Black Panthers, an African American political group of the 1960s. The Black Panthers worked to spread their message of African American power. Afeni and twenty other Panthers had been arrested on April 2, 1969. They were called the New York 21. The police said the group had planned to blow up several places in New York.

THE BLACK PANTHERS

The Black Panthers was a group founded by Huey Newton and Bobby Seale in Oakland, California, in 1966. Like Martin Luther King Jr., the Black Panthers fought for equality for African Americans. But they did not agree with King's nonviolent approach. When King and his followers were attacked during civil rights marches, they never fought back. But the Panthers believed in defending themselves.

The Black Panthers ran many useful programs. They gave free breakfast to poor children. They set up free health clinics in black neighborhoods. They also fought against police brutality. Sometimes, armed Black Panthers followed police officers around as they patrolled black neighborhoods.

Afeni Shakur began going to Black Panther meetings in 1968. She was twenty-two. Soon she became one of the few powerful women in the nearly all-male group. Afeni pushed for women to have an equal role in the party. For example, she wanted female Panthers to get weapons training just as the men did.

The Federal Bureau of Investigation (FBI) thought the Black Panthers were a threat. FBI agents joined the group to destroy it from within. Partly because of the FBI's efforts, the Black Panthers fell apart in the early 1970s.

While out on bail (money posted to get out of jail until trial), Afeni became pregnant. She was not sure who the father was. It may have been Billy Garland, another Black Panther. Or it may have been a local drug dealer, Kenneth "Legs" Sanders. At the time, Afeni was living with Lumumba

Afeni Shakur *(center)* and Black Panther members Elbert Howard *(left)* and Raymond Hewitt attend a press conference in the 1970s.

Shakur. Shakur was another member of the New York 21. When he found out she was pregnant by another man, he kicked her out.

Afeni helped raise bail for other members of the New York 21. But when two male members of the group left town, authorities sent her back to jail. Life at the New York Women's House of Detention was hard. Afeni had to get a court order so she could have one egg and a glass of milk every morning. She lost weight, but her baby kept growing. "I had never been able to carry a child past three months of pregnancy," Afeni said. "But in the midst of this, this child stayed."

Together, the members of the New York 21 were charged with 156 counts (crimes). They faced a combined 352 years in prison. Afeni served as her own lawyer, even though she had no education in law. Fearing the worst, she hoped her sister would raise her child. Instead, on May 13, 1971,

Demonstrators marched to free the New York 21 in February 1970.

TÚPAC AMARU II

Túpac Amaru II (1742–1781) was the last leader of the Incas. These people, native to Peru, were conquered by Spain in the 1500s.

Born José Gabriel Condorcanqui, Amaru later named himself after his great-grandfather. In 1780, he and his followers tried to defeat the Spaniards. The attempt failed. Amaru and most of his family were killed. But he became a famous symbol in the struggle for freedom.

Afeni and thirteen other members of the New York 21 were cleared of all charges.

On June 16, 1971, Tupac Amaru Shakur was born in New York. *Tupac Amaru* means "shining serpent." This was the name of a warrior in Peru in the 1700s. *Shakur* means "thankful to God" in Arabic. To Afeni, Tupac's birth was a miracle. "I knew, my gut knew, something about this child: that he wasn't supposed to be here. And he was!" she said later.

IT'S A FACT!

Afeni Shakur was born Alice Faye Williams. She was named after Alice Faye, a singer and movie star of the 1930s and 1940s. Afeni changed her name after joining the Black Panthers.

"And he was strong and he was . . . spirited and just the prettiest smile in the world. What a wonderful, wonderful spirit this child was right from the beginning."

It's a Fact!

According to some sources, Tupac's name at first was Lesane Parish Crooks. Afeni changed his name shortly after his birth.

CHAPTER 2
A YOUNG TALENT

BY THE TIME TUPAC WAS BORN,
Billy Garland was out of Afeni's life. Legs,
Tupac's other possible father, did not go away
completely. But for the most part, Afeni had
to raise her son alone. As a parent, Afeni did
not believe in hiding the truth. "She just told
me, 'I don't know who your daddy is,'" Tupac
said. (Tupac later accepted that Garland was
his father.)

At first, Afeni did well on her own. After her trial, she was treated like a minor star. She gave talks at Yale University and Harvard University. Later, she took a job at Bronx Legal Services in New York City. Afeni worked there as an assistant.

IT'S A FACT!
Afeni took Tupac to his first political speech when he was just days old.

In the mid-1970s, Afeni became involved with Mutulu Shakur. Mutulu was Lumumba Shakur's adopted brother. The couple did not marry. But Mutulu thought of himself as Tupac's stepfather. Afeni and Mutulu had a daughter, Tupac's half sister Sekyiwa (pronounced Set-chu-wa). Mutulu also had

GERONIMO PRATT

Tupac's godfather was Geronimo Pratt. Pratt was a high-ranking member of the Black Panthers. He went to prison in 1972 for murder and kidnapping. He claimed he had been falsely accused. Pratt's lawyer, Johnnie Cochran, fought for more than twenty years to free him. Pratt finally was freed in 1997 after his trial was ruled to be unfair. Some think his sentence was part of the FBI's efforts to destroy the Black Panthers.

Pratt could not be a real father figure to Tupac. He was in prison during Tupac's entire childhood. But he wrote Tupac many kind letters.

several other children. Among them was Maurice Harding, who later became the rapper Mopreme.

TEN-YEAR-OLD REVOLUTIONARY

Tupac showed creative talent early. He began writing plays when he was just six years old. He always wanted everything to be just perfect. He never let anyone else direct his plays. The actors (his cousins) had to follow his rules exactly. "He would have make-believe singing groups," Afeni said. "He would be Prince, or Ralph in New Edition. He was always the lead."

Tupac wrote poetry and love songs. He also kept a diary. "In that book I said I was going to be famous," he later said. He loved to read, a habit he picked up from his mother. When he was bad, Afeni sometimes punished him by making him read the entire *New York Times* newspaper.

Afeni joined the House of the Lord Church in Brooklyn when Tupac was ten. The pastor, Herbert Daughtry, once asked Tupac what he wanted to be when he grew up. He answered, "I want to be a revolutionary!" The Black Panthers was no longer an active group. But Tupac was still deeply moved by the views of his mother and the people she knew.

Around the same time, Mutulu had to leave the family to go into hiding. He was accused of working with others to commit armed robbery and murder. Mutulu claimed to be innocent. But he stayed on the FBI's Ten Most Wanted list for years. Possibly because of her link to Mutulu, Afeni lost her job at Bronx Legal Services. Afeni had not been rich before. But now she had to struggle to support her two children.

Afeni and the children moved often between the Bronx and Harlem, another part of New York City. At the worst times, they were homeless. All the moving around hurt Tupac deeply. Other kids

MUTULU SHAKUR

Mutulu Shakur is a political activist. He has been a member of the Black Panthers and other African American groups. In the early 1980s, the FBI put Mutulu on its Ten Most Wanted list. He was accused of an armed robbery that left two police officers and a security guard dead. Mutulu went into hiding for five years. He was captured in 1986.

Mutulu claimed he was a freedom fighter in the struggle for African American equality. He said the court had no right to try him. If a trial was needed, Mutulu said that he should be treated as a prisoner of war. Some experts agreed with him. But the judge rejected his idea. In 1988, Mutulu was sentenced to sixty years in prison.

bullied him. "I remember crying all the time. My major thing growing up was I couldn't fit in," Tupac said years later. "Because I was from everywhere, I didn't have no buddies that I grew up with. Every time I had to go to a new apartment, I had to [start over]. People think just because you born in the ghetto you gonna fit in. A little twist in your life and you don't fit in no matter what."

Legs lived with the family in the early 1980s. He spent time with Tupac. They would go to the barbershop or out for hamburgers. But Legs wasn't really a good influence. He was the one who first gave Afeni crack. She quickly became addicted to this powerful new form of cocaine.

Tupac was hurt by the lack of a steady father figure. His mother taught him how to cook, sew, and take care of a house. But she could not teach him how to be a man. "It made me bitter seeing all these other [kids] with fathers gettin' answers to questions that I have," he said. "Even now I still don't get 'em."

YOUNG ACTOR AND RAPPER

In 1983, when Tupac was twelve, Afeni signed him up with a theater group in Harlem. It was called the

The Apollo Theater is one of the best-know landmarks in the Harlem neighborhood of New York City. Many famous musicians have performed there.

West 127th Street Ensemble. The same year, Tupac made his first appearance onstage. He went onstage with the group at Harlem's famous Apollo Theater. He played Travis in the play *A Raisin in the Sun.* Tupac was the only child in the cast. At one point in the play, he was the only actor on the stage. Tupac loved the attention. But even more, he loved getting away from reality. "I didn't like my life, but through acting, I could become somebody else," he said.

Soon afterward, Legs went to prison for credit card fraud. Afeni and her children moved to White

IT'S A FACT!

Tupac's performance of *A Raisin in the Sun* helped raise money for Jesse Jackson's 1984 presidential run.

Plains, New York. There, they stayed in a hotel that was paid for by public aid. In 1985, they moved in with Afeni's cousin in Baltimore, Maryland.

When the family was settled, Afeni tried to contact Legs. But she learned he had died of a

A RAISIN IN THE SUN

A Raisin in the Sun is a play by Lorraine Hansberry. She wrote it in 1959. It was the first play written by an African American woman to be staged on Broadway in New York. *A Raisin in the Sun* is about a working-class African American family that buys a home in a white neighborhood. The play follows the troubles the family members have as they try to adjust to a new home.

The play reflects events from Hansberry's life. When she was a child, her family moved into Woodlawn, a white neighborhood on the south side of Chicago, Illinois. Hansberry remembered how unkind many of her neighbors were. Even as an adult, she felt very bitter about the experience.

heart attack from smoking crack. He was just forty-one years old. Tupac was angry about Legs's death. But he didn't cry about it for more than three months. "After he did," Afeni recalled, "he told me, 'I miss my daddy.'"

Tupac went to Rolling Park Junior High until eighth grade. Then he earned a spot at the famous Baltimore School for the Arts (BSA). He was one of the high school's few African American students. "That was the first time I saw there was white people who you could get along with," Tupac said. "Before that, I just believed what everybody else said: they was devils."

Tupac (upper left) poses with some of his friends, including Jada Pinkett (right), at the Baltimore School for the Arts.

He had several white girlfriends at BSA. For the first time, Tupac felt as though he fit in.

He also felt supported by the teachers, most of whom were white. Donald Hickens was the head of the school's theater department. He saw Tupac as a talented, serious actor. Hickens tried to do what he could to help him succeed. "For Tupac it was a new experience to be around white people who really cared about him," Hickens said.

Tupac enjoyed his classes. He read the plays of Shakespeare, took ballet, and went to Broadway shows. Even in a group of talented young people, Tupac stood out. "I loved going to school," he said. "It taught me a lot. I was starting to feel like I really wanted to be an artist."

One of his closest friends at BSA was dance student Jada Pinkett. They shared a painful bond. Pinkett's mother also used crack. Pinkett was shocked by how poor Tupac's family was. He owned just two pairs of pants and two sweaters. He slept on a mattress with no sheets. Many times, the fridge was empty and the electricity was shut off.

But Tupac had a small radio. In 1987, at the age of sixteen, he first heard "I'm Bad" by rapper LL Cool J. "I was writing rhymes by candlelight and I

The music of
LL Cool J fueled
Tupac's desire to
be a rapper.

knew I was gonna be a rapper," he said. Tupac's
first stage name was MC New York. He wrote his
first rap after a friend was shot. The song was about
gun control.

Tupac was doing well in Baltimore. But Afeni
was not. She had an abusive boyfriend. She used
crack often. In 1988, by the end of Tupac's junior
year, Afeni could no longer cope with her problem.
She sent Tupac and his sister to live in Marin City,

California. They moved in with a family friend, Linda Pratt. Tupac was sad that he had to quit BSA. "Leaving that school affected me so much," he said. "Even now, I see that as the point where I got off track."

IT'S A FACT!

Marin County is one of the richest places in California. But Tupac's new hometown of Marin City was an island of poverty within the county. The people there didn't share the rest of the county's wealth. Fewer than three thousand people, mostly African American, lived in the town.

3

THE JUNGLE

TUPAC'S NEW LIFE IN MARIN CITY,
nicknamed the Jungle, was hard. Once again, he
was the new kid trying to fit in. "It was like a
hood and I wanted to be a part of it," he said.
What he found was kindness but no respect. "I
got love but the kind of love you would give a
dog or a neighborhood crack fiend. They liked
me because I was at the bottom."

Afeni had sent her children to live with
Linda Pratt because Afeni wanted them to be
safe. But Pratt was an alcoholic. Sometimes

when she drank, she screamed at Tupac and Sekyiwa. When Pratt went into treatment for her alcohol problem, Afeni moved to California to look after her children. Life with Afeni was just as grim. Her crack use was out of control. Sometimes, she would disappear for months. She left her children to take care of themselves.

In the fall of 1988, Tupac began attending Mount Tamalpais High. Even though the school was in rich Marin County, Marin City itself was poor. Tupac had been a star at the Baltimore School for the Arts. But with his home life so unstable, he cut classes and let his schoolwork slide.

Tupac often stayed with friends rather than going home. Later, he moved in with a group of boys who lived in a vacant apartment. By this time, he was writing poetry and rap songs. His life was reflected in his lyrics. He recalled these dark days in the song "Dear Mama." According to the song, his mother kicked him out when he was just seventeen.

IT'S A FACT!

In his first videotaped interview, at the age of seventeen, Tupac spoke with a strong New York accent. His accent faded after a few years of living in California.

Tupac and his mother had little contact. "In New York and all those times we was growing up, she was my hero," Tupac said. But when crack took over Afeni's life, he lost all respect for her.

At the age of eighteen, Tupac dropped out of high school. But he kept reading. It was his way to educate himself. He pursued music, writing and rapping whenever he got the chance. He also listened to a wide range of music. He liked English and Irish pop. Among his favorite artists were Kate Bush, Culture Club, Sinead O'Connor,

Tupac enjoyed many kinds of music when he was a teenager including British pop singer Kate Bush (left).

Sinead O'Connor is an Irish singer and songwriter whose work Tupac liked.

and U2. He once said that his favorite piece of music was the theme song from the Broadway musical *Les Misérables.*

HIP-HOP DREAMS

The hip-hop scene in northern California was strong. It gave Tupac the chance to pursue his music. With new friend Ray Luv, Tupac formed a rap group called Strictly Dope. The two rapped at local clubs and house parties. They didn't make much money. But Tupac was writing and rapping. He was doing what he loved.

To make money, Tupac sometimes sold crack. But his Marin City friends—many of them drug

IT'S A FACT!

The recordings of Strictly Dope were released in 2001 under the name *Tupac Shakur: The Lost Tapes.*

dealers themselves—told him to stop. They saw Tupac's talent. They didn't want him to get caught up in the drug life. "I had so many loans from dope dealers, and I've never been able to repay because they're not here anymore," Tupac said. "They would just say, 'Here. Make that album. Mention my name.'"

Tupac wanted to break into the music industry. But he didn't know how. That changed in the spring of 1989. He had a chance meeting with Leila Steinberg. Steinberg, a young writer, teacher, and music producer, would become his first manager.

Steinberg was sitting in a Marin City park. She was reading a book written by Winnie Mandela. Winnie was the wife of antiapartheid leader Nelson Mandela of South Africa. To Steinberg's surprise, Tupac walked up to her and began quoting lines from the book. The two started talking.

Steinberg invited Tupac to a weekly poetry group that met at her house. Group members wrote, read, and discussed poetry. Tupac impressed

NELSON MANDELA AND APARTHEID

Apartheid is the word for the official policy of racial segregation in South Africa from 1948 to 1994. Nelson Mandela was a leader in the African National Congress, which fought apartheid. Because of his position, he was imprisoned for twenty-eight years, from 1962 to 1990. Four years after his release, Mandela became South Africa's first black president.

Nelson Mandela and his wife Winnie raise their fists in celebration as Nelson leaves prison in 1990 after twenty-eight years.

the group. "He was a genius who became the group's greatest inspiration," Steinberg said. When she found out Tupac was homeless, she offered to let him move in with her and her family.

THE ROSE THAT GREW FROM CONCRETE

Leila Steinberg kept Tupac's notebooks. They included the poems he wrote for her poetry circle. These early poems were released in 2006 under the title *The Rose That Grew from Concrete*. The book includes copies of Tupac's original notebook pages. The poems are printed in his own handwriting.

Tupac's friendship with Steinberg was based on a love of books and learning. "We searched for knowledge," she said. "We explored together."

Tupac went with Steinberg to local schools, where she taught her writing workshops. She taught, he rapped. "At seventeen," Steinberg recalled, "he was wide-eyed, and really believed that he could change the world."

Soon after their first meeting, Steinberg introduced Tupac to Atron Gregory. Gregory had started his own record label, TNT. Among his recording artists was the successful Bay Area rap group Digital

IT'S A FACT!

Tupac was a bad roommate, Steinberg once said. "He was the sloppiest, messiest person I've ever lived with."

Underground. Digital Underground's song "The Humpty Dance" was one of the first hip-hop songs played in clubs. It also became a number eleven hit on the pop charts.

Steinberg helped Tupac get a tryout with Digital Underground's lead rapper, Gregory "Shock G" Jacobs. At first, Shock G noticed Tupac's professional manner. Then, once Tupac performed for him, he was impressed with his rapping. "It was street. It was educated," Shock G said.

Tupac's early lyrics were either political or "hip-hop fantasy," Shock G said. An example of the hip-hop fantasy was the song "The Case of the Misplaced Mic." In the song, Tupac has to go to a rap battle without his beloved microphone. At the end of the battle, Tupac's opponent is dead. Then he finds that his mic was in his pocket all along.

In 1990, Tupac joined Digital Underground for their tour of the United States and Japan. He worked as a roadie. His job was to carry and set up equipment. He helped the band members in any way he could. He also danced onstage behind the main show. Tupac's duties included dancing with a life-size rubber doll during "The Humpty Dance."

DIGITAL UNDERGROUND

Digital Underground was one of the first hit rap groups from the West Coast. The band was known for its fun, adult party music.

Greg "Shock G" Jacobs was the lead rapper. He rapped in the band as himself and as Humpty Hump. Humpty Hump was a comic character who wore a fake nose and sang in a nasal style. During concerts, a silent stand-in would play either Shock G or Humpty Hump. Then after a noisy distraction, Shock G would switch roles.

Digital Underground's biggest hit was "The Humpty Dance." The song made it to number eleven on the pop charts.

REBEL OF THE UNDERGROUND

Tupac was happy to be dancing with Digital Underground. But he wanted to do more. "Every chance he get, he'd get on the mic—after the shows, at the after-parties," Shock G said. "Once people saw him, that was history."

Soon, Tupac earned the chance to do some background rapping (singing shorter parts to support the main rapper). He didn't like sharing the spotlight, though. Sometimes he would sing when he wasn't supposed to. Shock G would tell him to stop. Tupac would argue back. Shock G would kick him off the tour. Then the fight would blow over. Tupac would be back in the group as if nothing had happened.

Tupac's talent was obvious. But so was his temper. His new nickname was Rebel of the Underground. The name referred to his Panther background and his rebellious nature.

Tupac was small. He stood just five feet eight and weighed 150 pounds. Even though he wasn't big, he didn't avoid fights. Once, while on tour, Tupac got angry with the soundman for making a mistake. Tupac was just about to punch the man.

Tupac (left) performs with Digital Underground. Shock G is in the center as Humpty Hump.

Gregory held him back. "We were like, yo, Pac, you can't beat up the sound man!" said Ronald "Money-B" Brooks, Digital Underground's second rapper. "But he's crazy."

In 1991, Tupac had his first chance to rap on a record in the song "Same Song." As in much of Tupac's later work, the lyrics were about himself. He rapped about how girls didn't care about him before. But once he became famous, suddenly they did. Tupac's part in "Same Song" was short. But the other Digital Underground members were impressed by how much meaning he could pack in. Still, *Vibe* magazine's Danyel Smith wrote, "Tupac felt he had more to say."

"Same Song" appeared on Digital Underground's 1991 record *This Is an EP Release.*

VIBE

Vibe magazine was founded by musician and composer Quincy Jones in 1993. It was one of the first magazines to focus on hip-hop music, much like *Rolling Stone* and others focused on rock. After Tupac's death, *Vibe*'s editors collected the stories about him into a book, *Tupac Shakur: 1971–1996.* It was the first book *Vibe* had ever published. It became a best seller and appeared on the *New York Times* newspaper's Best Seller List.

An EP, short for "extended play," usually has five to eight songs. "Same Song" was also on the sound track for *Nothing But Trouble*, a film directed by Dan Ackroyd.

Nothing But Trouble was Tupac's first movie role. He and the rest of Digital Underground played themselves. In the film, the group is pulled over for speeding. They appear before a judge (played by Ackroyd). After they perform "Same Song"–with the judge joining in on keyboards–they are allowed to go.

Digital Underground's appearance was one of the highlights of *Nothing But Trouble*. But the film got bad reviews. "It's nothing but trouble and agony and pain and suffering and . . . bad taste," one reviewer wrote. Still, it was a start for Tupac.

BIG BREAKS

During this time, Tupac was writing and recording material for a solo album. He planned to release it under his stage name, 2 Pac. Gregory tried to convince TNT/Tommy Boy, Digital Underground's record label, to sign Tupac. But the label chose not to do so. Finally, the label Interscope took a chance on him. Tupac's debut album was set for release in November 1991. Tupac was twenty years old.

Around the same time, Tupac broke into acting. In late 1991, he was in New York touring with Digital Underground. Money-B had an audition for the film *Juice*, directed by Ernest Dickerson. Tupac asked if he could come along and try out too. Money-B didn't get a part. But Tupac was cast as Roland Bishop. It was an important supporting role.

Tupac's rapid successes in both music and acting meant a lot to him. But one simple goal was even more important. By the end of 1991, Tupac had earned enough money to rent his first apartment. Until then, Tupac had usually slept on

UNDERGROUND RAILROAD

Soon after he joined Digital Underground, Tupac started his own mentoring program, Underground Railroad. Once a week, Tupac spent time with a small group of young men. They read books, recorded raps, and went to movies together.

The original Underground Railroad was a secret network of people who helped slaves escape from the South in the 1800s. The name of Tupac's program paid tribute to that memory. It also honored Shock G of Digital Underground. "He had faith in me when nobody cared," Tupac said in 1991. "That's the most beautiful thing you can do for a human being."

the floors in band members homes. He even spent nights on recording studio couches.

Tupac's apartment was a small one-bedroom place in Oakland, California. At the time, parts of "Coke-land" (nicknamed because so many people there used cocaine) weren't safe. But Tupac was deeply proud of his new home. "Tupac showed us all around," Danyel Smith wrote in *Vibe*. He pointed out his new dishes, new silverware, new sheets, and towels. "[He was] telling us without telling us of his profound relief at having a place of his own." Tupac had put up with years of being homeless. Having a home of his own meant more than he could say.

CHAPTER 4
A Thug's Life

Tupac's first solo album, *2Pacalypse Now*, hit record stores late in 1991. The album title was a cross between his stage name and the 1979 film *Apocalypse Now*. The word *apocalypse* refers to "the end of the world." *2Pacalypse Now* showed the influence of Digital Underground's members. They had helped Tupac make the record. One song was titled "Rebel of the Underground," his Digital Underground nickname. Another song, "Trapped," featured Shock G as a background rapper.

But Tupac's solo material was different from Digital Underground's goofy party songs. *2Pacalypse Now* was clearly influenced by N.W.A.'s album, *Straight Outta Compton*. Like *Straight Outta Compton*, *2Pacalypse Now* was gangster rap. It was full of angry rhymes about urban life. It also took aim at the police.

IT'S A FACT!

Apocalypse Now, directed by Francis Ford Coppola, was a 1979 film about the horrors of the Vietnam War (1957–1975). It appealed to Tupac, who wanted to show people the horrors of urban life.

"Trapped," for example, accuses the police of singling out black men. In the song, Tupac raps that black men can hardly walk around without the police going after them. In the song's chorus, Tupac repeats over and over again that "they" have him trapped.

Tupac's first single, "Brenda's Got a Baby," was even bleaker. It tells the story of a twelve-year-old girl who gets pregnant. After she gives birth, she throws the baby in the garbage. When the baby cries, Brenda comes back and brings it home. But her family soon kicks her out. Brenda tries to support her child by selling crack. Later, she sells

STRAIGHT OUTTA COMPTON

Straight Outta Compton, released in 1988 by N.W.A. (Niggaz with Attitude), is thought of as the first gangster rap album. The songs were too violent to be played on the radio. The Federal Communications Commission (FCC) controls what kind of content can be broadcast on public airwaves. N.W.A.'s music was too harsh for FCC standards. But even though the music wasn't on the radio, the album still sold more than three million copies.

herself for sex. In the end, she is murdered.

The song was very powerful. Many wondered if it was about someone Tupac knew. "No, she ain't somebody I know," he told *Vibe*. "She's one a them girls we all know." "Brenda's Got a Baby" made it to number three on the rap charts. The song helped *2Pacalypse Now* go gold (sell more than five hundred thousand copies).

IT'S A FACT!

The music industry gives honors to artists based on the number of albums sold. A gold album sells five hundred thousand copies or more. A platinum album sells one million or more. For two million copies sold, an album gets double platinum status. For three million, triple platinum.

TRAPPED

When Tupac wrote "Trapped," he had never been arrested or harassed by police. But that changed in the fall of 1991. On an October day, police stopped Tupac in downtown Oakland. They had seen him jaywalking (crossing the street against the light). At first, Tupac gave the police no problems. He showed the officers three forms of ID. But the two officers did not believe Tupac Shakur was his real name.

Oakland is a city close to San Francisco. Both cities are on San Francisco Bay.

Tupac began to lose patience. He asked why it took two officers to stop him for jaywalking. Oakland, after all, had a high rate of serious crime. Jaywalking didn't seem like that big of a deal. Finally, Tupac lost his temper and swore at the officers. They put him in a choke hold and knocked him to the sidewalk. "I woke up cuffed up, with my face in the gutter with a gang of people watching me like I was the criminal," he recalled.

Tupac spent seven hours in jail before the police released him. He missed the debut of his video on the popular hip-hop television show *Yo! MTV Raps.* In December of 1991, Tupac filed a $10 million lawsuit against the Oakland police. The case was settled for $42,000.

"No Place in Our Society"

Tupac was still just twenty years old when his first film, *Juice,* came out in January of 1992. His character, Bishop, was a troubled man with anger problems. In the film, Bishop gets a group of friends to rob the corner store. Things go wrong when Bishop shoots and kills the store's owner. The film got mixed reviews. *The Washington Post* called it "passable but rather routine." But several critics noted Tupac's strong performance.

Tupac enjoyed the fame he got from *2Pacalypse Now* and *Juice*. "I loved the fact that I could go to any ghetto and be noticed and be known," he said. But his success in *Juice* had a bad side. He had played the part so well that many people began to think he wasn't acting. Tupac was not just a gangster rapper, they thought. He must be an actual gangster.

In April of 1992, Tupac's gangster image began to cause him problems. A young man in Texas, Ronald Ray Howard, shot and killed a state trooper. Afterward, officers found a copy of *2Pacalypse Now* in Howard's tape deck. Howard was facing the death penalty. To save Howard's life, his lawyer tried to blame Tupac. He claimed that Tupac's music had caused Howard to shoot the trooper. The lawyer singled out one lyric from "Soulja's Story." In the song, Tupac raps that he would rather shoot a cop than let one shoot him.

A few months later, Vice President Dan Quayle spoke out against Tupac's music. He said *2Pacalypse Now* was helping to destroy U.S. values. Quayle asked Interscope to pull Tupac's album from store shelves. "This music has no place in our society," he said. Tupac was amazed that Quayle even knew who he was.

In time, Tupac decided to embrace his new gangster image. Gangster rap was more popular than ever. Rap based on political issues was less popular. Twenty-one-year-old Tupac responded to this shift and helped make it happen.

In one interview, Tupac compared his lyrics to the television coverage of the Vietnam War. The Vietnam War was the first conflict to be shown on television news in the United States. The U.S. public had never watched real war as it happened. Many scholars have claimed that the U.S. reaction to the TV coverage helped turn people against the war. Similarly, Tupac said, "I'm going to show the most graphic details [of ghetto life] and hopefully they'll stop it—quick."

KEEPING IT REAL

Tupac had never been in a gang when he was growing up. He often said that before he made a record, he never had a record. By this, he meant he hadn't had a criminal record. But the line between his life and his art was blurring. In the hip-hop world, authenticity—keeping it real—was important. Many of Tupac's fans expected him to get into trouble.

When he moved to California, Tupac had dressed like the art student he'd recently been. But as he became more famous, he adopted a tougher look. His style included a head rag, sweatshirt, low-slung jeans, a nose stud, earrings, and a Rolex watch. In 1992, Tupac had *Thug Life* tattooed on his stomach. The *i* in *Life* was a rifle bullet.

CULTURAL GRAFFITI

Tupac had many tattoos. Most famously, the words *Thug Life* were inked in large letters across his stomach. *Outlaw* and Christ with a crown of thorns were on his right arm. A snake was on his right shoulder. *Playaz* was on the back of his neck. A German cross with *Exodus 18:11* ("Now I know that the Lord is greater than all gods . . .") was across his back. There were many more.

One critic compared Tupac's back to how record samples sound. He pointed out that ideas, like the music, overlapped and bumped into one another.

Tupac also collected guns. "You can't survive out here by yourself," he said. "The police ain't nothing but a gang. The National Guard is a gang. The army is a gang. . . . Somebody get a gun, the government get a bigger gun."

In August of 1992, things took a tragic turn. Tupac returned to Marin City for its fiftieth-anniversary festival. He got into a fight with some people in his old neighborhood. The conflict ended in gunfire. No one directly involved in the fight was hurt. But Qa'id Walker-Teal, a six-year-old boy playing in a nearby school yard, had been shot and killed by a stray bullet from the fight.

Tupac had not fired the gun. But the boy's family still filed a lawsuit against him and Interscope. The case was settled out of court for a reported $300,000 to $500,000. Tupac later said the shooting haunted him. He deeply regretted being part of the accident.

"Tupac felt that he had to live the life that he sang about in his songs," Dyson said in the film *Thug Angel*. "That's great when it's applied to gospel music, terrible when it's applied to gangster rap."

"It's not that we have the answers because we don't," Tupac said about himself and other gangster

THUG LIFE

Tupac often called himself a thug and said he was living a thug life. He said this was due to Legs's influence. "That's where the thug in me came from," he said. In response to his critics, he claimed that he didn't invent thug life.

With his stepfather Mutulu Shakur, Tupac wrote the "Code of Thug Life." The code included twenty-six rules for thugs. (In this context, *thug* seems to mean "gang member.") It banned selling drugs to children or pregnant women. It forbade harming civilians or the elderly. The code also stood against helping the police.

Tupac's mentoring program, Underground Railroad, eventually turned into a musical side project called Thug Life. He worked with young rappers from all over. In the early days, these included many from the East Coast.

rappers. "We're just being who we are, being as truthful to ourselves as we can. It's beyond good and evil. It's a thug life."

DRIVEN TO SUCCEED

Tupac started to feel guilt about having gotten out of the ghetto when other people couldn't. His guilt only made him work harder. He would write and record three or four songs a day, sometimes more.

"If something happened to him, he wanted to write about it right on the spot," Money-B of

Digital Underground said. The rapper Notorious B.I.G. (Christopher Wallace) said that Tupac once got up to go to the bathroom. When he came back, he had written two raps.

Writing lyrics "was his air. That was his oxygen," Shock G said. If Tupac was unhappy with what he had written, he would not change it. He'd throw it out and start a new song. "He just poured it out. . . . He came in there and said it how he felt it."

But Tupac didn't have the best work habits. He needed to be drunk, high, or both to write songs. Tupac's drugs of choice were marijuana (weed) and alcohol. At the time, Tupac did not believe he was addicted. But his old friend Jada Pinkett was not fooled. "His mind was never clear," she said.

Tupac's drug use also changed his vocal style. He smoked so much in the studio that he often gasped for breath and skipped words. Tupac's solution was to triple his vocals. He would record the same song three times. Then he'd mix (overlap) the three recordings. That way, every word was clear.

A SECOND ALBUM

Tupac's second album, *Strictly for My N.I.G.G.A.Z.*, came out in February 1993. Like other gangster

rappers, Tupac used the "n-word" often. Unlike
other rappers, Tupac changed the ugly word. He
turned it into an acronym, "N.I.G.G.A." He said it
stood for "never ignorant, getting goals
accomplished." *Strictly for My N.I.G.G.A.Z.* went on
to sell more than one million copies.

**Tupac raps for an
audience in 1993.**

The songs on *Strictly for My N.I.G.G.A.Z.* were
just as conflicted as the title. Its biggest hit, "Keep
Ya Head Up," was a salute to black women,
especially single mothers. In the song, Tupac gave a
shout-out to women on welfare. He said he cared
about them, even if no one else did.

According to Danyel Smith of *Vibe*, "On each
of Tupac's albums, he included at least one song
that [showed] the side of himself that believed in
good." Despite its grim viewpoint, "Brenda" was the
"good" song of *2Pacalypse Now*. "Keep Ya Head Up"
was the "good" song of *Strictly for My N.I.G.G.A.Z.*

But other songs on the album undercut this
good message. "I Get Around" was about
irresponsible sex. The song featured Shock G and
Money-B from Digital Underground. But the very
next track, "Papa'z Song," shows a child's view of
this behavior. In the song, Tupac rapped that his
mother was the only one who stuck around. His
father had left them with no money. Tupac's
stepbrother, Mopreme (son of Mutulu Shakur),
rapped with him on the song. Mutulu had left both
of them during the years he hid from the FBI.

"Everybody got a good side. Everybody got a
bad side," Mopreme said. "Just Pac's was amped up

a little bit more." Many of Tupac's friends and fans shared Mopreme's view. But Tupac did not. "People who think I'm like two different people—a wild gangsta and a caring, sensitive young black man—don't really know me," he said.

Meanwhile, Tupac's behavior continued to make headlines. In March of 1993, he was arrested for threatening a limousine (limo) driver in California. In April, he was jailed for ten days in Michigan for attacking a local rapper with a baseball bat.

POETIC JUSTICE

Tupac's second film was supposed to have been *Menace II Society*. The film was about a young man trying to survive the rough housing projects of Watts, a neighborhood in Los Angeles, California. The directors of *Menace II Society* were young twin brothers Allen and Albert Hughes. They had made some of Tupac's videos. But after Tupac had several fights with them, they kicked him out of the cast. Tupac claimed they didn't even inform him personally. He first heard about his firing on MTV.

Tupac was angry. He stormed the set of a video that the Hughes brothers were filming. Armed once again with a baseball bat, he went

IT'S A FACT!

Menace II Society was the feature film debut of Tupac's old friend from BSA, Jada Pinkett. Pinkett later appeared in films such as *Ali* and *The Matrix Reloaded*.

after both twins. "That's a fair fight, am I right?" Tupac said. "Two [people] against me?" He was arrested for assault. Allen Hughes also filed a lawsuit against him. Once again, it was Tupac's behavior—not his talent—that was making headlines.

Instead of *Menace II Society*, Tupac's second film was *Poetic Justice*. It came out in July of 1993. Tupac had just turned twenty-two. Singer Janet Jackson played the lead character, named Justice. She's a hair stylist who dreams of becoming a poet. Tupac's character, Lucky, is a mail carrier and single father who wants to be a rapper.

Poetic Justice was director John Singleton's second film. Singleton was exactly the type of director Tupac wanted to work with. His first film, *Boyz N the Hood* (1991), had been nominated for two Oscars. Like the Hughes brothers, Singleton was a young African American. He made movies about the inner city. On the set, Tupac's relationship with

Director John Singleton grew up in south central Los Angeles. His movies are often drawn from his childhood.

Singleton was similar to the one he had with Shock G. "We'd argue, then make up," Singleton said.

Tupac's character, Lucky, was the male lead. But Tupac thought the character was poorly written. In speaking his lines and giving his performance, he tried to give Lucky the depth that

IT'S A FACT!

Poetic Justice featured an appearance by the well-known African American poet Maya Angelou. She is also the author of the poetry that Janet Jackson's character writes in the film.

Tupac and his costar Janet Jackson on the set of *Poetic Justice*

the script lacked. Many critics noticed. "Shakur's Lucky is movingly complex," Robert Faires wrote in the *Austin Chronicle.* "In his shrugs and sighs are the hundred wrestling feelings of a man with dreams fighting to hang on."

Janet Jackson was well aware of Tupac's rough past. She had asked that he take an AIDS test before filming their on-screen kiss. Tupac was hurt that Jackson would be worried about catching AIDS from him. (Casual kissing does not lead to

AIDS.) Perhaps because of that demand, the costars had no spark. Still, the film got mostly good reviews. One *Washington Post* writer called it "often graceful, sometimes brilliant." For the positive role he played, Tupac was nominated for an Image Award by the National Association for the Advancement of Colored People (NAACP). It was a new experience for a self-proclaimed thug.

5 FROM PRISON TO DEATH ROW

BY 1993, TUPAC WAS ONE OF RAP'S

biggest stars. As his popularity grew, so did his police record. Still, he had never been accused of a serious crime. Ten days was the longest jail sentence he had ever served. But in the space of three weeks, that changed.

His manager had noticed that Tupac's life was getting out of control. He had talked Tupac into buying a home in Atlanta, Georgia. This southern city is a center for African

American business, politics, and music. Tupac
agreed that the slower, calmer pace of life in the
South would be a good change.

But the change didn't work out as planned. On
October 31, 1993, just days after moving to Atlanta,
Tupac was arrested again. This time, the charge was
serious—aggravated assault. He was accused of
shooting brothers Mark and Scott Whitwell. They
were both off-duty police officers.

The Whitwells claimed that after a traffic
dispute, Tupac opened fire. Tupac argued he had
stopped his car after he saw the Whitwells
harassing an African American driver. When one of
the officers drew a gun, Tupac fired in self-defense.

Soon the Whitwells' story began to fall apart.
Several witnesses said Mark Whitwell had been the
first to pull a gun. Worse still, the Whitwells' guns
had been stolen from a police locker. Both officers
may have been drunk. And in their report on the
incident, they had used a racial insult to describe
Tupac and his friends. Seven months after the
shooting, Mark Whitwell quit the force. The
charges against Tupac were dropped.

After this shooting, many of Tupac's fans
thought of him as almost superhuman. Not only

had he shot two white police officers, he had gotten away with it. He had not even gone to trial. That was hard to believe. "Shooting cops? And living to tell the story? And beating the rap? He was beyond real," Danyel Smith wrote in *The Vibe History of Hip Hop.*

EAST COAST VS. WEST COAST

Hip-hop was born in the early 1970s in New York. But in the early 1990s, gangster rap, which came out of California, began to take over. Los Angeles began to rival New York as a hip-hop capital.

An East Coast-West Coast rivalry began to develop. It was worse between New York's Bad Boy Records (run by Sean Combs) and L.A.'s Death Row (run by Marion "Suge" Knight). At first, the rivalry was mainly about money. But after Tupac was shot and mugged in 1994, the rivalry turned personal. Tupac claimed Combs and the Notorious B.I.G., who was signed to Bad Boy, had set him up. Before the shooting, Tupac and Biggie had been friends. There was never any proof for Tupac's claim. But he believed it. The shooting and mugging was never solved.

The rivalry grew worse after Biggie released the single "Who Shot Ya?" Biggie said the song was not about Tupac. But Tupac thought Biggie was making fun of him. In response, Tupac released the single "Hit 'Em Up" with his new side project, the Outlawz.

By the mid-1990s, the rivalry was almost as bad as gang warfare. Produce and rapper Andre Young (Dr. Dre) saw that the bad feelings were getting worse. He said, "Pretty soon [people] from the East Coast ain't gonna be able to come out here and be safe. And vice versa."

MORE TROUBLE

A few weeks later, Tupac made the news again. He was in New York working on a basketball movie called *Above the Rim*. On November 14, 1993, Tupac met a nineteen-year-old woman at a dance club. Several days later, the woman came to visit Tupac at his hotel. What happened after that is unclear. The woman later told police that Tupac and three friends had raped her. Tupac did not deny that she had been raped. But he said that he had left the room before the rape occurred.

The alleged rape of a young woman in 1993 happened at this hotel in New York.

Tupac was arrested. He was charged with several crimes, including sexual assault and sexual abuse. On the night of his arrest, he was defiant. "I'm young, black. . . . I'm making money and they can't stop me," he said. "They can't find a way to make me dirty, and I'm clean."

Once again, Tupac was front-page news. Many of the articles spoke out against Tupac and gangster rap. "For years, these rappers have been preaching drug culture and violence," a California politician

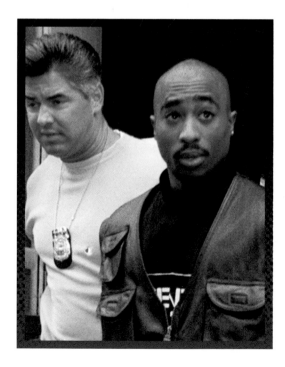

Tupac (right) was arrested on November 19, 1993, in Manhattan.

said in a *New York Times* article. "But now they are openly living that life style. . . . That will have a [bad] effect on our young people who [imitate] the way these rappers dress, talk, and act." Similarly, the headline of a *Newsweek* article asked, "When is Rap 2 Violent?"

Kevin Powell of *Vibe* saw things from Tupac's viewpoint. "I look at Tupac and I see myself, my homeboys, all the brothers I've ever [known], trying to prove ourselves to the world," he wrote. "But I wonder why Tupac's efforts . . . are so destructive. Over the past several months, as the media reported one violent incident after another, many people asked, 'Is Tupac on a self-destructive mission? Does he have a death wish? Is he crazy?'"

Tupac was released on bail. He was set to stand trial the next year. At the same time, John Singleton had planned to cast the twenty-two-year-old Tupac as the lead in his next film, *Higher Learning.* Singleton and Tupac had already worked together once, on *Poetic Justice.* After Tupac's arrests in Atlanta and New York, producers forced Singleton to drop him. Tupac's gangster image helped sell gangster rap records. But it did not work in Hollywood.

In March 1994, *Above the Rim* was released. Tupac's character, a drug dealer named Birdie, was "a standard cliché," reviewer Roger Ebert wrote in the *Chicago Sun-Times.* However, Ebert wrote, "Shakur plays him well, and he makes a satisfactory bad guy."

TUPAC SHOT

Tupac was twenty-three when his sexual assault trial began in November of 1994. He faced up to twenty-five years in prison. Tupac said that he was innocent. He claimed that the police were out to get him because of his antipolice lyrics. During the trial, Tupac's lawyers blamed his accuser for what had happened.

Meanwhile, Tupac was running short of money. His records were still selling well. But he had lawyers to pay. And because of all that had happened, many of his concerts had been canceled. Tupac started

IT'S A FACT!

In 1990, Afeni realized that her crack use was out of control. She moved back to New York and managed to kick her habit. She was clean by the time she went to work for Tupac in 1994.

Tupac listens during his 1994 trial.

hiring himself out to rap on other rappers' records
to earn extra money.

On the night of November 29, Tupac and
three friends stopped by Quad Recording Studios.
He had agreed to record a verse for the young East
Coast rapper Little Shawn. Tupac felt nervous about
it because he didn't know the rapper well. But he
needed the fee.

In the lobby of the building, two men pulled
out guns. They shouted at the group to lie on the

floor and give up their jewelry. Tupac grabbed for one of the guns. The men shot him five times. He was hit twice in the head, once in the left arm, once in the thigh, and once in the groin. Then the attackers took his diamond ring and gold chains.

His friends dragged Tupac into the elevator and up to the studio. First, Tupac wanted some marijuana. He smoked it and called his mother as his friends tried to slow down the bleeding. Then he called 9-1-1.

The police arrived quickly. Among them was Craig McKernan, who had arrested Tupac for the rape the year before. Tupac said hello and called

THUG LIFE VOLUME 1

Thug Life, Tupac's side project with young rappers, released its first album in October 1994. The lyrics on *Thug Life: Volume 1* were even darker than Tupac's solo material. "*Volume 1* shows only one side of the so-called gangsta [mind]: getting paid and avenging for dead homies [close friends]," Cheo Hodari Coker wrote in *Vibe*, "There's little that [shows] the futility of all that violence, or the daily stresses that lead countless kids down this path."

Thug Life: Volume 1 was planned to be the first of a series of Thug Life albums. Tupac's plan was for the members of the group to change. He wanted to give unknown rappers their first big break. But for many reasons, no more albums were made.

the officer by name. "Hey, Tupac, you hang in there," McKernan said.

OVERNIGHT RECOVERY

When Tupac awoke in Bellevue Hospital Center, he had another shock. "After I got shot, I looked up and there was this [person] who looked just like me," Tupac said. Sitting by his bedside was Billy Garland. The men looked so much alike that Tupac was sure Garland must be his father.

Garland had seen Tupac's face on a movie poster for *Juice*. The face on the poster was a mirror image of his own. When he heard about Tupac's shooting on the news, he came to visit. It was the first time Tupac and Garland had met.

Tupac was afraid that the attackers would come back to the hospital to finish him off. He had bodyguards posted outside his door. All the next day, Tupac continued to bleed heavily. At 1:30 P.M., he had surgery on his right leg to stop the bleeding. The surgery was over at 4 P.M. At 6:45 P.M., he checked himself out of the hospital against the advice of his doctors.

The next morning, December 1, Tupac showed up at his trial. The jury had no contact with the

outside world. So they didn't know that Tupac had
been shot. He didn't want them to think he was
skipping a court date. "I knew I had to show up no
matter what," he said. Tupac arrived in a
wheelchair. His left wrist was bandaged. His
bandaged head was hidden under a knitted hat. His
bandaged leg was under sweatpants.

**Tupac had to use a
wheelchair to come and
go from court, but he
did show up the day
after his shooting.**

Later, Tupac left the courtroom because his leg
went numb. He needed medical help. He secretly
checked into a different hospital under the name
Bob Day. Despite his efforts to hide, he continued
to get death threats by phone.

Tupac was too sick to return to court that day.
He wasn't there when the jury gave its verdict.
They found Tupac guilty of sexual abuse. But he
was cleared of the more serious sexual charges and
of weapons charges. The judge sentenced him to
one and a half to four and a half years in prison.

Tupac always claimed he had not raped the
woman. However, he was sorry that he hadn't done
something to stop the rape. He said he should have
made sure any woman in his hotel room was safe.

Tupac's overnight recovery from five gunshot
wounds became legendary. The fact that he had
been shot during his trial confirmed the ideas of
both critics and fans. "For those who want gangsta
rap off the market, he was living proof of the genre's
[hatred of women] and violence," Jon Pareles wrote
in the *New York Times*. "But for fans, he became the
[perfect example] of street-tough 'realness.'"

Others in the hip-hop scene were not so sure
this "realness" was very real. "He has portrayed the

role of thug," Jeremy Miller of *Source* magazine said. "There's a line where it's reality, and not reality. I think he's right on the line."

PRISON

Tupac began serving his sentence at Clinton Correctional Facility in Dannemora, New York, on February 14, 1995. He had always believed that at some point he would serve time in prison. Afeni,

A guard tower of the Clinton Correctional Facility. Tupac served his sentence at this prison in 1995.

Legs, Mutulu, and so many others he knew had served time. As a young man, he had even told Leila Steinberg that prison would give him good material for his raps.

But the reality of prison was nothing like his fantasy. He went through bad withdrawal symptoms when he stopped smoking marijuana. The other inmates harassed him. One rumor said that Tupac was sexually assaulted in prison. In an interview with *Vibe*, Tupac strongly denied it.

Once he had been able to write four songs a day. In prison, he couldn't write lyrics at all. But he did write a screenplay called *Live 2 Tell*. It was about a drug lord who struggles to change his life.

IT'S A FACT!

On April 29, 1995, Tupac married girlfriend Keisha Morris at the prison where he was serving time. Tupac had met Morris, a prelaw student, at a New York club in 1994. The marriage was later legally dissolved as if it had never existed. "I moved too fast," Tupac told *Vibe* in February of 1996. "I can only be committed to my work or my wife. I didn't want to hurt her. She's a good person. So we just took it back to where we were before."

Before he went to prison, Tupac told Jada Pinkett that he was going to give up thugging. He planned to get rid of all his guns and get a new set of friends. He even thought he might give up rap and focus just on acting.

In a famous prison interview with *Vibe*, he made similar promises. "Thug Life to me is dead," he said. "If it's real, then let somebody else represent it, because I'm tired of it. . . . This Thug Life stuff, it was just ignorance. My intentions was always in the right place."

Tupac also talked about how his lyrics affected others. "If you see everybody dying because of what you saying, it don't matter that you didn't make them die," he said. "It just matters that you didn't save them."

ME AGAINST THE WORLD

While Tupac was in prison, his third album, *Me Against the World*, was released. The album had been recorded before Tupac went to prison. It debuted at number one on one of *Billboard's* music charts. Tupac became the first singer to have a number one album while serving time in prison. Despite his situation, Tupac thought of the success of *Me Against the World* as "one of my career highs."

Many critics have pointed to the paranoia (fear not founded in reality) that runs through Tupac's work. *Me Against the World* was the best example yet. In "Death around the Corner," Tupac admits what the cause might be. Smoking weed, he rapped, was making him paranoid. (Paranoia is a well-known side effect of smoking weed, or marijuana.) Tupac did have real reasons to feel fear. But drugs clearly made his fears worse.

Like most of Tupac's work, the album was partly about him. The first sounds on the album are pretend news reports of his shooting. In another song, he raps that he is not a rapist. A *New York Times* reviewer wrote about how real Tupac's work was. "As other rappers strive to prove their 'realness,' 2Pac has become a [true] outlaw, with bullet wounds and . . . prison sentence to prove it."

The most famous single from the album is another one of his "good" songs. "Dear Mama" is a thank-you to Afeni for her hard work as a single mother. One critic pointed out that Tupac speaks more clearly on "Dear Mama" than any other song.

It is as if he doesn't want his listeners to miss a single word.

The track's most famous lyric is also its most honest. In it, Tupac calls his mother a crack fiend as well as a black queen. In those two lines, Tupac declares his love for Afeni as well as his disappointment in her. Like his mother had been, Tupac was brutally honest.

"Dear Mama" was the main reason that *Me Against the World* sold two million copies. It also showed his fans—especially his female fans—that he was not the monster the media said he was. Tupac was serving time for sexual abuse. But "Dear Mama," like "Keep Ya Head Up," showed a softer side.

DEATH ROW

Tupac's lawyers tried to get him released while they asked a judge for a new trial. But he could not raise the $1.4 million he needed for bail. That was when Marion "Suge" Knight, the head of Death Row Records, stepped in.

Knight visited Tupac in prison. He brought a contract to join Death Row Records. Knight offered to post the $1.4 million bail. The money was an advance on royalties (Tupac's share of the profits) on future albums. In exchange, Tupac would release three albums on the Death Row label. Tupac signed the deal. Tupac always said that he wanted to be on Death Row Records. But some people close to him felt that he had no choice in the deal.

DEATH ROW

Death Row Records was co-founded in 1992 by Knight and Andre Young *(right)*. Young was a member of the original gangster-rap group, N.W.A. Knight and Young had been childhood friends.

Death Row's first release was Dr. Dre's *The Chronic* in 1992. By 1995, *The Chronic* had sold more than two million copies. In three short years, Death Row had become the biggest rap label in the country.

Knight was a smart, talented businessman. But he ran Death Row in a strange, sometimes violent way. In his office, he kept a fish tank with piranhas—aggressive meat-eating fish. He liked to feed them mice or rats. Knight had been convicted of various crimes, including assault with a deadly weapon. In 1995, he was given five years' probation for beating two rappers with a gun as a punishment for using a studio phone. There were stories of many other violent incidents.

On October 13, 1995, twenty-four-year-old Tupac walked out of prison. Knight sent a private jet to fly him back to California. That same night, Tupac was in the studio to record new music. By the next day, he had finished seven songs for his next album.

Tupac spent many hours working at a sound mixing board like this one.

Tupac's work ethic hadn't changed. But something else had. Many of his old friends noticed the difference. "The light and the wit, the way that he would shine, it was completely changed, dimmed after that experience," Leila Steinberg said.

Prison time had not given him endless material for raps, as he had hoped. Instead, Tupac told Steinberg, "Jail killed my spirit. It wore me out. I'm tired now. I don't know if I'm making any difference."

CHAPTER 6

Tomorrow Is Not Promised

TUPAC INSISTED HE WASN'T GUILTY of
sexual abuse. And while in prison, he seemed to
truly want to change his image. But after he
signed with Death Row, all of his promises went
away. Tupac's gangster image was worse than
ever. Few of his fans or friends were surprised.
Tupac's messages had always been in conflict.
He had also always longed to fit in. His
membership in Death Row was the closest
Tupac had ever come to being in a gang. And if
he wanted to be in the gang, he had to act like
he was in the gang.

In an interview with a San Francisco radio
station, Tupac said he had learned in prison that
he couldn't change. "You know how they say,

Tupac (left) and Suge Knight lived the thug life.

'You've made your bed, now lay in it?' I tried to move. I can't move to no other bed. This is it."

All Eyez on Me, Tupac's first album for Death Row, made his new commitment to the thug life clear. Prison hadn't made him a better person, Tupac rapped on "No More Pain." In fact, he had become even worse. The song ended with him shouting about thug life and the west side, meaning the West Coast.

IT'S A FACT!

All Eyez on Me is often called the first rap double album. But this honor actually goes to DJ Jazzy Jeff and the Fresh Prince's *I'm the DJ, He's the Rapper*, released in 1988. The Fresh Prince is now better known as actor Will Smith. He is married to Jada Pinkett Smith.

All Eyez on Me was a double album. It included twenty-seven songs and was more than two hours long. The album featured more than a dozen guest rappers. Tupac said he named the album *All Eyez on Me*, "because they are. Everybody's watching for me to fall, die, get crippled, get AIDS, something."

Me Against the World had showed the gangster life as self-destructive. But *All Eyez on Me* celebrated it. Tupac raps about driving fancy cars, drinking, smoking, and chasing women. "2Pac glamorizes the gangster life for anyone who'll buy the fantasy," Pareles wrote in the *New York Times*.

The album also renewed the East Coast-West Coast rivalry. On the cover, Tupac uses three fingers to make the W hand sign. He later said that the W stood for "war." *All Eyez on Me* included the song "Wonder Why They Call U," with backup vocals by Faith Evans. Evans was Biggie's wife. To get at Biggie, Tupac said that he and Evans had had a sexual relationship. Evans strongly denied it.

The album went on to sell more than ten million copies. But not all critics liked it. One *Vibe* reviewer wrote that the album sounded "slapped together." He added, "*All Eyez on Me* is not the crime Pac has actually been convicted of, but it's pretty bad."

FRANTIC PACE

As ever, Tupac didn't just rhyme about the thug lifestyle. He also tried to live it. "Tupac . . . liked to stir up stuff and then watch it explode in others' faces," Dr. Dre said. "That's a hard way to live and a quicker way to die."

Tupac was living life on his own terms. But to his old friends, he didn't seem to be enjoying his success. "He wasn't so happy," Shock G recalled. "A lot of his laughter was forced. All those records, all he's talking about is the pain."

According to Gobi, Tupac's friend and video director, Tupac surrounded himself with people. Yet, at times, he seemed to be very much alone. "Tupac seemed happiest when he was on a set or in the studio," Gobi wrote in his book, *Thru My*

Tupac takes time to sign an autograph at a charity event in the mid-1990s.

Eyes: Thoughts on Tupac Amaru Shakur in Pictures and Words.

Tupac was working at a frantic pace. He would shoot a movie during the day. At night, he'd work on a video. He and Gobi shot six big-budget music videos in a few months. Sometimes Tupac was so tired he would sleep in the limo between locations. If Tupac had any extra time, he would go to the studio. He recorded hundreds of tracks during this period.

Tupac wanted to fulfill his contract with Death Row as soon as he could. He wanted to start his own projects. Gobi wasn't surprised. He said that people like Tupac are always in a hurry because they "know that tomorrow is not promised."

In public, Tupac expressed only deep loyalty to Death Row and Suge Knight. Tupac's relationship with Knight was almost like that of a father and son or of brothers. Knight often spoke of Death Row as being like a family.

Tupac finished three films after he got out of prison. All of them centered on the drug trade or drug use. In *Bullet* (1996), he played another bad-guy dealer. In *Gang Related* (1997), he and Jim Belushi played crooked cops who rob and murder

Jim Belushi was Tupac's costar in *Gang Related* (1997).

drug dealers. In the black comedy *Gridlock'd* (1997), he and Tim Roth played drug addicts trying to quit.

Meanwhile, Tupac was setting up some projects of his own. He founded a film company, called 24/7, with Gobi and another partner. Tupac also set up his own production company, Euphanasia. The name combined the words *euphoria* (joy) and *euthanasia* (mercy killing). He even had plans to start his own record label, Makaveli Records.

TUPAC'S BOOKS

Tupac read all the time. He left high school without a diploma. But he had read more books than many college graduates.

Before his death, Tupac left his books with Steinberg. Among his collection are:

The Art of War by Sun Tzu

The Catcher in the Rye by J. D. Salinger

Dictionary of Cultural Literacy: What Every American Needs to Know by E. D. Hirsch

I Know Why the Caged Bird Sings by Maya Angelou

In Search of Our Mother's Gardens by Alice Walker

The Life and Words of Martin Luther King Jr. by Ira Peck

The Meaning of Masonry by W. L. Wilmshurst

Moby Dick by Herman Melville

Native Son by Richard Wright

The Odyssey by Homer

The Prince by Niccolo Machiavelli

Roots by Alex Haley

Sisterhood Is Powerful: An Anthology of Writings from the Women's Liberation Movement edited by Robin Morgan

The Souls of Black Folk by W. E. B. Du Bois

Tears and Laughter by Kahlil Gibran

Zen and the Art of Motorcycle Maintenance: An Inquiry into Values by Robert Pirsig

TROUBLE IN VEGAS

On September 7, 1996, Tupac was in Las Vegas for a boxing match between Mike Tyson and Bruce Seldon. The bout, held at the MGM Grand Hotel, lasted just two minutes. At 8:39 P.M., Tyson knocked Seldon out.

At about 8:45, Tupac, Knight, and others from Death Row got into a fight of their own. Shortly after the match, they scuffled with Orlando Anderson. The reasons for the fight are unclear. Some people think Anderson was a member of a Los Angeles gang. He may have beaten up one of Tupac's bodyguards a few weeks before. Hotel security quickly broke up the fight. Tupac and his group left the building.

Later, Tupac met up with Knight to go to his nightclub, Club 662. Tupac and Knight drove in Knight's 1996 black BMW. Ten other cars filled with Death Row employees and friends trailed behind them.

At about 11:15 P.M., Knight's car stopped at a red light at East Flamingo Road and Koval Lane. A white Cadillac pulled up along the passenger side. Someone in the white Cadillac fired thirteen shots into Knight's car.

Tupac tried to climb to safety in the back seat. But he was hit four times. Two bullets hit him in the chest, one in the hand, and one in the leg. Knight made a U-turn and tried to flee. But he hit a road divider. Soon the police arrived. An ambulance took Tupac and Knight to the University Medical Center. Knight was treated for minor injuries to his head and was released.

IT'S A FACT!

Tupac sometimes wore a bulletproof vest. But he left it off the night he was shot in Las Vegas.

The car Tupac was riding in when he was shot was taped off by police so they could investigate.

At first, news reports about Tupac's condition differed. An Associated Press report said that his life wasn't in danger. Many of his fans thought Tupac would pull through. He had already survived the New York shooting, as well as a gun battle with Atlanta cops. Why should this time be any different?

STRUGGLE FOR LIFE

Over the next two days, Tupac had two surgeries. The first was to remove his right lung. The second stopped internal bleeding. On the third day, the doctors prescribed drugs to put him into a coma. They did so because he kept trying to get out of bed.

Gobi, Tupac's director

Gobi wrote about his visit to Tupac's hospital bed. "I saw his bandaged body covered by a thin white sheet, with tubes and machines . . . all over. Bandages covered his bullet wounds, and one of his fingers was missing. His head was swollen as a result of all the [drugs] they had pumped into him. I walked over and put my hand on his arm. It was cold. I said a prayer and walked silently out of the room."

For seven days, Tupac fought for his life. Outside the hospital, a crowd of well-wishers came and went. Rumors about the shooter ran wild. Some people thought the shooter may have been Anderson, the man Tupac and his friends had fought with at the MGM Grand. But hotel security staff had been talking to Anderson at the time of the shooting. Others thought Knight might have been the real target. But all the shots had been aimed at the passenger side. Another idea was that Tupac was killed as a warning to Knight or to get even with him. Yet another theory was that Tupac's shooting had come out of the East Coast-West Coast rivalry. The crime has never been solved.

Knight and other members of the Death Row group were of little help to the police. No one

IT'S A FACT!
Six months after Tupac's death, the Notorious B.I.G. was shot and killed in Los Angeles. He was twenty-four years old. Biggie's murder has never been solved. His second album, *Life after Death*, came out two weeks after his death.

had seen the shooter. They'd only seen the white Cadillac. No one had seen its license plate number. And no other witnesses came forward with clues. "They were not quite [open]," Sergeant Kevin Manning of the Las Vegas Police Department said about Knight and his friends.

Rumors among the crowd gathered outside the hospital said that Tupac was getting better. For seven days, Tupac clung to life. But at 4:03 P.M. on Friday, September 13, he lost the fight. The official

AN UNEXPECTED RELATIONSHIP

Tupac sometimes spoke out against other famous people for no good reason. In one interview, he attacked musician and producer Quincy Jones. He said that Jones should not have married a white woman, actress Peggy Lipton.

Their daughter, Rashida, wrote a letter to Tupac asking for an apology. At a party, Tupac mistook her sister, Kidada (right), for Rashida. He went over to say he was sorry. They started talking, became friends, and later fell in love. At the time of his death, Tupac and Kidada were engaged to be married.

cause of death was a heart attack combined with breathing trouble.

Afeni Shakur chose to have her son's body cremated soon afterward. She didn't hold a funeral. Only a small private service held in Las Vegas took place. Tupac's family and friends later spread his ashes in the Pacific Ocean near Los Angeles.

7 RESURRECTION

Tupac's
death
inspired
someone to
paint this
tribute on a
garage
door.

TUPAC'S DEATH HIT HIS FANS HARD.

For weeks, reporters were writing stories about it. The *New York Times*, for example, ran three major articles about Tupac on three separate days.

Tupac's death meant different things to different people. To fans who understood his